LET'S GO TEAM:
Cheer, Dance, March

19.95

LET'S GO TEAM:
Cheer, Dance, March

COLOR GUARD
Competition

Terry Usilton

Mason Crest Publishers
Philadelphia

Mason Crest Publishers, Inc.
370 Reed Road
Broomall, PA 19008
(866) MCP-BOOK (toll free)
www.masoncrest.com

First printing

1 2 3 4 5 6 7 8 9 10

Library of Congress Cataloging-in-Publication Data

Usilton, Theresa A.
 Color guard competition / Theresa A. Usilton.
     v. cm. — (Let's go team — cheer, dance, march)
Includes index.
Contents: Macy's Thanksgiving Day Parade — The history of color guard
— Color guard — Winter guard — Pageantry arts.
 ISBN 1-59084-537-4
1. Marching drills — Juvenile literature. 2. Color guards — Juvenile literature.
[1. Marching drills. 2. Color guards.] I. Title. II. Series.
 GV1797 .U75 2003
 791 — dc21

Produced by
Choptank Syndicate and Chestnut Productions
226 South Washington Street
Easton, Maryland 21601

Project Editors Norman Macht and Mary Hull
Design Lisa Hochstein
Picture Research Mary Hull

Printed and bound in the Hashemite Kingdom of Jordan

OPPOSITE TITLE PAGE

Color guard members use their bodies and flags to express emotion and add visual interest to a band's performance.

Table of Contents

The Macy's Parade

They had been standing out in the cold for hours waiting to begin a "once in a lifetime" experience. They had been practicing since 2 A.M. Now, in the predawn darkness, the Mighty Sound of Maryland marching band was ready to proceed down the route of the 74th annual Macy's Thanksgiving Day Parade. Streetlights brightened the November morning and uniform sequins sparkled as the University of Maryland color guard and band members marched to take their place in the parade lineup. Soon, accompanied by twirling rainbow flags, they would play a customized version of "Over the Rainbow" for 20 million television viewers and parade spectators.

The 74th Macy's Thanksgiving Day Parade works its way through New York City on November 23, 2001. The University of Maryland's marching band was one of only 14 bands chosen to participate in the 2001 parade.

The performance was the culmination of a long application process. Each year bands apply to the New York department store to be in the parade. Using videotapes and recordings, Macy's auditions the applicants. Of the 14 bands appearing in the 2001 parade, the Mighty Sound of Maryland and Ohio University's bands were new, while the Bergenfield High School band from New Jersey was making its 20th appearance.

Maryland color guard section leader Alicia Williams felt "really, really excited" when her band was accepted. Then she realized, "It's going to be a lot of work." Dr. L. Richmond Sparks, director of the Mighty Sound of Maryland, said he felt "happy, excited, and lots of pressure for a televised event."

The University of Maryland's band is known for its creative marching formations and choreography. The color guard's role is auxiliary. "They make the music flow," said Dr. Sparks. Their program choreography was done by Suzanne Sturgis, a former member of the band's silk line who returned to be its instructor. The 10-foot flags attached to $5^{1}/_{2}$-foot PVC poles, along with the guard's smooth, precise choreography, make the Mighty Sound of Maryland a visual as well as audio pleasure.

The color guard joins more than 200 instrumentalists to form the marching band. In choosing band and guard members, Dr. Sparks looks at their skill and potential. In order to perform at parades, games, and other events, the entire group normally practices two evenings a week. Getting ready for the parade increased the practice time for everyone. Parade practices were held in addition to

The Mighty Sound of Maryland performs with other bands on the field during halftime at a University of Maryland football game.

practices and performances for the regular marching season and football games because Macy's wanted advance videotapes of what their performance would be like.

Adjustments had to be made. They were used to performing on a field that had lines to give them landmarks for turns and other moves. On the street they would have no guidelines, so they practiced on an unmarked field. They also had to make sure their program could be performed in a smaller area. New York streets are narrower than football fields. They practiced for months, sometimes very early in the morning or late in the evening, no matter what the temperature, in order to give their best performance.

As they perfected the music and learned choreographed marching formations, Dr. Sparks guided the band from his position on a cherry-picker platform 35 feet in the air. This high vantage point let him see any holes in the formation. He used the loudspeaker system in the stadium to call out orders. Students were told to speed up or slow down so that they would be moving together.

Thanksgiving Day finally arrived. By the 9 A.M. starting time, the Mighty Sound of Maryland was lined up along with clowns, floats, balloon handlers, other bands, and huge helium balloons. An estimated one million people lined the parade route. "I've never seen so many people," said Alicia Williams. The enormous crowd pumped the marchers with adrenaline. They didn't feel the cold weather anymore.

The University of Maryland's marching band was given an enviable marching position in the very middle of the parade. This was great placement because by mid-parade the viewing audience is at its peak. Because of the need to coordinate with the television network's schedule, the band had lots of starts and stops as they

INSIDE THE MACY'S PARADE

Lining up for the Macy's Thanksgiving Day Parade occurs in several different areas. Bands line up in one area, floats in another, balloons in yet a different spot. This procedure can mean that performers from one area really see very little of the parade they are in. Depending on their position in the lineup, some performers won't even see the giant balloons.

waited for earlier entertainment groups to perform. With television cameras trained on them, the band and color guard performed to their huge audience. Alicia had told all of her friends to watch for her, but she knew that it would be hard to pick her out since all band members wore the same uniform. "You didn't really know when the camera was on you," she said. One of the best parts of the broadcast was being able to see it again later and realize that the part the color guard had been working on the hardest had been taped and looked great.

Since much of their performing emphasis during the year was on promoting school spirit, the Mighty Sound of Maryland members were used to smiling a lot. Spectators commented that it seemed as if they were the only band who smiled and seemed happy and excited to be there. Alicia said, "I love hearing that kind of feedback from the spectators because we're there to entertain, and we're there for them."

When their two-minute television spotlight ended, the band continued to march down the remainder of the parade route. The memory of the sounds, the people, and their performance will last a lifetime. Alicia summed it up, saying, "It was a lot of work and pretty stressful, but it was a wonderful experience. It's nice to be able to say I marched in the Macy's Parade."

The Sport of the Arts

Carrying flags to show allegiance to a country or group is not a new concept. Flags have been around since about 3,000 B.C. when they were used in China for military and religious purposes. These flags, made of silk, were usually attached to one side of an upright pole. In wartime, ancient peoples such as the Egyptians used streamers tied to poles to see which way the wind was blowing so that their arrows would be more effective. During the Middle Ages some flags were so large, they were placed on carts to be taken to the battlefield.

In a battle each side or group had a flag to show the generals where their soldiers were. Knights often

Twirling flags and elaborate rifle and saber drills are the hallmarks of color guard.

Color guard has military roots. Historically, military units designated a member who carried their flag. Here students at the Marine Military Academy perform a rifle drill, with the color-bearer in the background.

placed small flags called pennons on their lances to help in their identification, which was made difficult by their armor. Battles centered around the flag, and defending the flag was one of the main obligations of a soldier. If the flagbearer was injured, another soldier was expected to take the flag and continue carrying it. Soldiers would rally around the flag to protect it. If the flag was captured by an enemy, soldiers would often give up the fight.

Flagbearers were accompanied by people playing drums, pipes, and horns. These instruments helped troops know where to move and provided a beat for marching. Flags had been used for centuries as signals in battle, but in the 14th century the Swiss also began using drums, a practice that was adopted by many European countries.

The person who carries the national flag is called the color-bearer. In military or patriotic organizations, a color

COLLEGE COLOR GUARDS

Many colleges and universities offer opportunities for guard members and other performing artists. The Indiana University Flag Corps is part of the university marching band, known as the Marching Hundred. The flag corps says that while their routines might seem simpler than the ones used by high schools, they have a different show for every game, sometimes learning the routines in only two days. As part of the Kent State University Marching Golden Flashes, the color guard helps lead the cheers for the football team. As the Kent State Web site says, "[Spectators may] listen to the band, but they're watching the guard!" The Purdue All-American Flag Corps performed at a recent Rose Bowl. The Blue Band Silks from Penn State University start game day practices five hours before kick-off. The night before their last home game, the silks, majorettes, and feature twirler take turns on stage in Bandorama, the band's performance of the music from the season's halftime shows.

Drum corps combine color guard with percussion and brass instruments, building on the traditional association between flag bearers and drummers, pipers, and horn players.

guard often has a color-bearer, two escorts, and another member who carries the organization or unit flag. The national flag will be on the right of the other flag, with an escort on the side of each of the two flag bearers. In a parade with a line of other flags, the color-bearer marches in front of the others at the center of the line.

During the first half of the 20th century, color guards in America included an American flag, possibly a sponsor flag (such as the organization's or unit's flag), and two persons with either rifles or sabers as escorts or "guards." Later, additional flags called guidons were used to mark intervals between company squads. As each corps presented its colors, usually with a patriotic tune in the background, the American flag was brought forward and saluted.

In the years immediately following the 1914–1918 World War, former soldiers celebrated the Fourth of July and Armistice Day (now called Veterans' Day) by marching in parades that featured drums and bugles, the same instruments and rhythms that generations of soldiers had marched to. Drum and bugle corps evolved, such as the all-male corps of the Veterans of Foreign Wars (VFW) Post 342 and American Legion Post 62 in Rockford, Illinois.

In 1956 the VFW Post 342 corps became a competitive drum corps called the Phantom Regiment, with an all-girl color guard called the Phantomettes. By 1970 the group included a 24-person color guard and 10 rifles. The Phantom Regiment continues to compete and place well in competitions, including the annual Drum Corps International (DCI) World Championships.

TWIRLERS ADD TO THE SHOW

Baton twirling sections, often seen as part of a band front along with the color guard, were added to marching bands in the 1930s to increase audience appeal. Drum majorettes were often the only females in the band. That situation changed in the 1970s, when legislation required that all girls be offered equal sports opportunities in schools receiving federal funds. Women became more involved in marching band, color guard, and the other pageantry arts.

Over time, drum corps routines departed from their strictly military origins and added classical, contemporary, and jazz music, as well as tunes from Broadway musicals. While the presentation and guarding of the national flag remained important in military and patriotic ceremonies, the music being played became more varied. As the music choices grew, so did the role of the visual ensemble, the color guard.

Sometime in the 1970s, this ceremony began to be embellished by swirling the flags in the air. Elaborate rifle and saber drills followed. As more variations were introduced, color guards looked for ways to outdo each other, leading to competitions.

Increasing competitions led to the 1971 creation of Drum Corps International to establish the rules for competitions. Based in the United States, DCI's influence extends to parts of the Far East, Western Europe, and Africa. The formation of DCI has been credited with a great increase in the sophistication of creative and artistic skills in color guards and drum and bugle corps.

Color guard is visual enhancement for the marching band. Modern guard members include drama and facial expressions in their performance. While some groups use the terms interchangeably, color guard and winter guard are two separate, but similar, entities. Color guard is associated with marching bands and outdoor performances; winter guard is performed indoors, often to pre-recorded music. Color guard generally uses brighter colors and bigger moves for its larger performance area. Some high school and most college color guards use different

The 1947 Baltimore Colts Marching Band poses for a group photo. In the first half of the 20th century, the only openings for women in marching bands were as baton twirlers, also known as drum majorettes.

flags depending on the halftime programs. Flags can be changed for individual performances. It is not unusual for a color guard to use four or five flags in one halftime show. Ribbons and hoops with streamers are also used. Occasionally, the flags may be changed during different sections of the same number.

Winter Guard International (WGI) is an international organization that promotes the pageantry and performing arts, including all aspects of guard competition.

In addition to flags, props used in both color (outdoor) and winter (indoor) guard include decorative rifles and sabers. Guard members must have strong upper bodies in order to master their performance with these weapons.

Both color guard and winter guard require a great deal of practice and stamina. Color guard takes a lot of dedication because guard members often practice every day and work on their skills in all kinds of weather.

While color guard and winter guard participants may use a variety of props, including hoops and streamers, there are three main pieces of equipment: flags, rifles, and sabers. Flags (also referred to as silks), come in specified sizes for competition. Swing flags may be no longer than three feet; field flags are much larger. All guard members should be capable of performing with this basic piece of equipment.

Rifles are made of wood and are usually painted white. They have no firing mechanism. Though rifles can vary in size and weight, they are rather heavy and represent strength and power. They can be difficult to handle as they spin faster and there is more impact when they are caught.

The saber is a sword with a hardened plastic or metal hilt and a steel blade. The edge of the blade is either dulled or sheathed by wrapping tape or cloth strips around it. Many color guard members who handle sabers wear gloves for added protection.

Color guard competitors must be in good physical shape. Each piece of equipment has physical requirements. Flags require strength in the forearms and wrists because the poles are 5 1/2 to 6 1/2 feet long and can be heavy. Six-foot poles are becoming more popular because larger flags can be hung from them to enhance visual impact. Color guards perform under all weather conditions, and a rain-soaked flag is difficult to maneuver.

Basic flag moves begin with right shoulder and left shoulder marching, just as flags were carried when color guard first began. A tricks class teaches advanced moves that serve as crowd-pleasers. These moves, which include catching flags in an unusual place such as the upper leg, or rotating the flag around the guard's waist, are not generally used in a parade performance.

The saber is the smallest piece of color guard equipment and the hardest to catch. Though it is more difficult to use, its sleekness and the fast-paced, graceful movements of its performers make it a visual pleasure. Members who perform with sabers usually have ballet training. Foot movement is more demanding and their programs include dance, difficult turns, and jumps.

Stanley Knaub, a founder of WGI, has pointed out that bigger, longer, and heavier equipment has returned, such as 7-foot flag poles with 3 x 5-foot flags. These dimensions are the same as were originally set forth by the American Legion and VFW standards. Sometimes rifles can be too long or heavy for a more petite member of the guard to maneuver smoothly. During competition, a person who is not quite strong enough to perform necessary moves may compensate by a slight twist or dip of the body before lifting or tossing the equipment. Since a group is judged on the effect and precision of its program, it is more important for the performers to have a smooth, professional appearance than to have heavier and bigger equipment than their opponents may have.

In addition to a unity of movement, there must also be a visual appeal to a guard. Costume design is a big factor. A costume should depict a role or character, adapt to the stage area (taking into account color and distance), and provide freedom of equipment. Many considerations must be taken into account, including performers' sizes, body shapes, and budget. The color of the performance area must be considered; dark blue costumes on a black floor, for example, could detract from the program's appearance. Performance designers advise guard instructors to be aware of the impact they want to make and be sensitive in choosing costumes that will enhance the visual impression and facilitate the performers' movements to result in a unique approach.

Costumes and uniforms are very important to color guards. The image which a color guard or drum and bugle

Winter guard, which is performed indoors with props and sets, is one of the fastest growing pageantry arts.

corps or any other pageantry arts group wants to project, the subject of its program, and the group's historical background all have an influence in its choice of clothing. Just as flags were identified with a group on the battlefield, a color guard's uniform sets it apart from its competitors.

Color Guard

Color guard is a component of a marching band or drum and bugle corps in which performers extend the musical program and entertain spectators mainly through the use of flags, rifles, and sabers, although streamers, hoops, and other equipment or props may also be used. The Edmonton Ambassadors Colourguard Ensemble of Alberta, Canada, describes color guard as fun and innovative dance using equipment to create a "highly visual and entertaining show" through interpretation of music. The modern color guard is not only a precision marching unit, it often serves as a dance ensemble and storyteller.

Guard members must use precision timing and movement to synchronize their motions to the music that is being played.

Some color guards require established skills levels from candidates auditioning for their groups. Often the requirements depend on the group's size and competition level. By 2001, the Blue Devils of Concord, California, had finished among the top five corps of Drum Corps International for 27 consecutive years, and they had won the DCI World Championship 10 times. By January of each year the group has narrowed its approximately 1,000 applicants to 64 brass players, 36 color guard dancers, and 28 percussion players. The Blue Devils attract international members from countries such as England, Canada, and Japan.

The marching band from Council Rock High School in Newtown, Pennsylvania, specifies that members be able to dance, use multiple equipment, and fly silk flags. This group also requires band camp, along with attendance at football games, rehearsals, exhibitions, and competitions. Other groups have a more lenient policy for beginning guard candidates. The Edmonton Ambassadors say, "No experience is necessary to join this ensemble, but if you do, be prepared to learn lots, work hard, travel, meet new people, and have lots of fun."

Color guards are usually composed of both male and female members. Guard instructor Anthony Nolley, also a member of the Northern Lights Winter Guard in Portland, Oregon, has been spinning, or performing with twirling flags, since he was seven or eight years old. He teaches the tricks class of more intricate color guard competition and performance moves and specializes in saber. Anthony says that when other people hear what he

The color guard adds visual interest, color, and movement to a band's performance. They can tell a story with their bodies, using facial expressions and dance as well as props.

does, their usual response is "cool" because they do not have his skills.

Color guard members, along with the rest of their group, know what few of the spectators realize—that their seemingly effortless performance of spinning flags and rifles or moving with precision is the result of hundreds of hours of hard work and rehearsing. Some of the routines, incorporating choreographed marching, dramatic costuming, and mesmerizing flag movement, take months to achieve.

Not only do the band and color guard help carry on a tradition of entertainment at sporting events, especially football games, they are intense competitors who strive for perfection. "If you don't do it perfectly, then you messed up," says color guard captain Jordan Dudney of McLean High School in Virginia.

Every detail matters in a champion color guard. Jessica Allen of the Blue Devils says, "Eating correctly, being respectful of others, pushing through the smallest details in choreography, and conducting yourself in a professional, mature manner are just a few of the key elements that bind the greater picture."

Competition is an important factor in the life of a color guard member. Tournaments and competitions are held locally, regionally, and nationally. Competitions often involve long bus rides and sometimes airplane rides to national and international events. Much of this travel occurs on weekends. The Blue Devils tour across the country every summer. The team travels by bus on a six- to eight-week tour and usually sleeps in sleeping bags on the gym floors of the schools where they perform. They get up, rehearse, perform, pack up, drive to the next place and follow the same routine. "It's a road show," says the group's executive director, David Gibbs. The Blue Devils have also spent weeks in European countries such as Holland, France, and Germany.

The Edmonton Ambassadors Colourguard Ensemble has traveled around the world, and performed at the Rose

Bowl and Disneyland. Other color guards have journeyed to South Africa for drummies competition—a mixture of aerobic sport, dance, and rhythmic gymnastics that includes competition in single flag, double flag, and twirling flag.

Color guard, marching band, and corps competitions create much pressure to perform well. Participants make a strong commitment to practice and rehearse long hours. Austin Allen, a drum major for the Spirit of Stonewall from Manassas, Virginia, uses at least 20 hours each week to help the group prepare for the weekend sports events and competitions. It is a great deal of responsibility to keep members on task, teach drill, and teach the show. "But when it all comes together, it's worth it," he says.

Becoming a guard member involves auditions. The highly competitive corps are more demanding of their members. Early fall is usually the time for tryouts, after the corps' summer season has ended and there is a short break in their schedules. It is possible to join a corps'

DAZZLING PERFORMANCES

The Boston Crusaders' 2002 "You Are My Star" program included the corps ensemble singing while guard members carried poster-sized pictures of famous Americans such as Albert Einstein, Jackie Robinson, Martin Luther King Jr., and Marilyn Monroe. For a finale, most of the members lie on the field to create a red, white, and blue formation of the American flag.

Effective choreography is important in color guard competition because it creates smooth transitions that help guard members follow the music and synchronize their performance.

color guard in winter after practice has begun, but it's almost impossible to do so during the summer when the group is touring and competing.

Auditions may extend over several days, often on a weekend. During that time, there will be sessions using movement and equipment. The candidates for the guard will have several chances to show both their skills and their attitudes. For the Pacific Crest Color Guard of Diamond Bar, California, the second day's tryouts include an informal interview. Even returning members have to audition yearly. During the auditions, the staff looks at the attitude of the candidate toward learning and performance, basic technique, equipment handling, how well and quickly moves are learned and mastered, body control, and how well the rhythm's beat is followed.

Being chosen to become a color guard member is only the first step. Next comes a series of practices and camps to learn the music and moves. A pageantry arts group needs its members to work with each other, not try to outshine each other. Judging is based not only on how well they perform together, but on how well each member's talents blend with those of other team members. Preparation includes a series of rehearsals and camps held periodically during the year to refine the skills and techniques used in a program.

The Boston Crusaders Drum and Bugle Corps requires attendance at a camp every month during winter. Weeknight sectionals are added in May, with a required attendance at a regional camp that includes an intensive three- to four-week rehearsal schedule of 10 to 14 hours per day.

The Irondale Marching Knights in Minnesota begin practicing in May and continue until the end of the school year in June. Rehearsals then extend from mid-July until the end of the show season in November. Included are a May day camp, two off-site mini-camps, a week-long evening camp at the high school, and a week-long field show camp in August, where the Marching Knights prepare for their competitive field show.

The West Coast Sound Drum and Bugle Corps is based at Oceanside High School in California. The corps, which features a rifle and flag squad, practices all summer. Their director, Gary Backlund, says, "We teach them work ethics. They learn to work as a team and they think about their music 24 hours a day."

Colleges and universities offer summer camp opportunities, as do independently-run camps and clinics. For example, the University of Kansas holds a summer camp focusing on guards, drum majors, and leadership. The guard camp covers all aspects of flag and rifle technique, and includes instruction on marching technique, equipment and color selection, dance movement, and coordinating routines to music. A typical guard camp day starts at 8 A.M. and can continue until after 9 P.M.

"During the summer I work harder than I do any other time of the year," says Blue Devils color guard member Jennifer Byers. "Being in the sun [all day] tests your personal strength and limits. At times it's monotonous, emotionally draining, and even physically painful."

Injuries are a common result of practice. The equipment is not sharp, but it is heavy. It can be painful if the rifle, sword, or flag lands on the performer in a way that was not planned. But dedicated performers like Angela Rudow of the Ventures Colour Guard Teams of Canada say that the bruises and long practices are worth it. "It's so much fun. You get this feeling in your gut," she said. Her friend Jacqueline Karley added, "Suddenly you can be whatever you want to be. I love it."

Musical selections chosen for competition programs vary greatly. The junior Ventures, ages nine to 13, practice their routine to a variety of popular songs. A senior

While their routines may seem effortless, guard members often practice for months in order to coordinate the use of props with marching, dance, and music.

Ventures' routine was based on the *Moulin Rouge* movie soundtrack. The Highlights Flag Team of Illinois performed a routine based on the *Titanic* movie soundtrack. Other competitive groups are known for their focus on jazz, Broadway, or classical music.

Many performance arts competition groups are large. Generally these include color guard and winter guard ensembles, drill and dance teams, marching bands, twirling groups, and drum and bugle corps. Competitions are also geared to individuals, partners, or small groups. Competition categories are based on levels of experience, size of the performing group, or both. In this way, groups with similar criteria compete fairly against each other.

Tournament of Bands (TOB) is one of the largest band competition organizations in the nation, with performance opportunities in field band, indoor guard, majorette, percussion, and dance team. It has a scholastic or single school-unit category and an independent division in which the performers may come from different areas and not all attend the same school.

The youngest participants in TOB's color guard events are the Elementary class (through grade six if school-based) or Cadet (through age 10 if independent). These two classes do not compete, but receive ratings of their performances. Competitive classes are Middle (through grade nine) or Junior (through age 14), Novice, World, University, and Senior. The Novice entry-level competition assesses beginner skills in movement and handling of flags and weapons. Novice Class A competition recognizes that the members may be young or less experienced, but have skill development above entry level. Novice Open class is the most advanced of the Novice designations. The World class is the highest level with the most advanced programs. Innovation is one of the qualities assessed. These color guard units must have the talent,

THIS COLOR GUARD GETS AROUND

The 45-member color guard of the Southwest Missouri State University Pride Marching Band has performed in three Macy's Thanksgiving Day Parades, the Tournament of Roses Parade, the Lord High Mayor's New Year's Day Parade in London, England, and at Disney World and Disneyland. It has also been the feature band at the Bands of America Grand National Championships.

instructional staffs, and budget required for a World class unit. The University class designates participants enrolled in a single college or university, and the Senior class is for members age 23 and older.

For Tournament of Bands, guards must have at least five performing members, and no more than 30. Timing is very important. Groups have time limits for performance, equipment, props, and presence on the performance area. Performance times are determined by class, with the least experienced participants (elementary/cadet) given 3 to 5 $1/2$ minutes, and World class participants having 4 to 7 $1/2$ minutes. There are limits to what guards can do in their performances. Any use of flammable or otherwise dangerous materials or the use of live animals results in instant disqualification in all classes. The individuals in the group are judged on their movement and equipment elements (20 points for each), and the entire group is judged as to its effect as an ensemble or group (20 points). Additionally, two judges may award up to 20 points each for the general effect of the performance to determine the score from a total of 100 possible points.

Judges for these competitions are often past participants in the events that they are judging. In order to stay qualified, judges have to participate in mandatory training workshops to stay current with the expectations and requirements of the competition they are judging. The National Judges Association was founded for the advancement and education of its members in judging all pageantry-oriented events, and to promote youth involvement in these arts through school and independent

Drum Corps International, Winter Guard International, and marching band organizations like the Tournament of Bands offer a variety of competitions for color guards.

opportunities. Judges can be certified for Tournament of Bands, Winter Guard International, and Drum Corps International on state, national, and international levels, as well as for judging drill teams, cheerleading, and parades.

Drum Corps International holds World Championships each summer in three divisions. Division I is for drum corps having up to 135 members. In order to be ranked in this division, the corps must have placed in the top 25 at World Championships and be capable of extensive touring. Division II ranges from 61 to 128 members. This division participates mostly in regional and local events and tours on the weekends. Division III may have up to 60 members. It competes mostly on local and regional levels.

In addition to these competitions, there are many other circuits and associations that organize or take part in competitive events. Bands of America, the Michigan Color Guard Circuit, the North Texas Colorguard Association, the Northwest Pageantry Association, and the Southeastern Color Guard Circuit provide news on upcoming competitions, results, and the names of competing groups in their area.

Regardless of the outcome, competitors discover that success is not always measured in terms of winning. Blue Devils color guard captain Jessica Allen says, "Winning is a bonus when you are a part of a great color guard. The most magical part of the 2001 Blue Devils Color Guard was the spirit we each had."

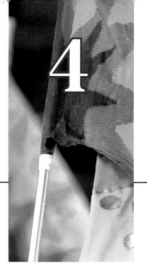

Winter Guard

When the regular marching band and color guard season is over, it's time for winter guard. Winter guard is different from color guard because it can be performed to live or taped music, and it is performed indoors. Unlike color guard, winter guard cannot exceed a total of 30 guard members and musicians combined. The guard Web site Silkonline.org describes winter guard in this way:

> Groups utilize their unique mixture of bodywork, theatrics, and equipment work to illustrate a chosen piece of music. The music may tell a story, set a mood, or express an idea.

The Northview High School Winter Guard performs in the Scholastic World Class division at the 2002 Winter Guard International World Championships held in Dayton, Ohio.

Either way, the senses are bombarded by the final product. Most importantly, winter guard is a place where performers can come together to form a team and learn from one another as they build self-confidence and improve themselves as people.

Winter guard auditions are usually held in September. Guard members from the previous year may be required to audition also. Rehearsal clothes, equipment, and indoor and outdoor shoes are usually brought to an audition. An advanced division is looking for more skilled members, while a novice division will be more likely to offer training in basic moves. Some guards state that the most important attributes of all are positive attitude and willingness to learn. Since winter guards in the Independent divisions are not restricted to members from a certain area, some applicants who live in other states send videotapes for their auditions. Northern Lights Winter Guard recommends that audition tapes include basic moves and skills that the applicant is comfortable performing, along with clips of past performances. They also want to hear why the applicant wants to join the guard.

Becoming a color guard or winter guard member can be expensive. Membership fees or tuition can range from less than $100 to over $1000. The Pacific Crest World Guard 2002 has a fee of $1400. The King's Renaissance Winter Guard fees range from $200 to $300. Fees alone seldom cover all expenses for facilities, instructors, costumes, equipment, and travel, so guards participate in fundraising activities. The bingo sponsored by Northern Lights Winter Guard is so successful that it does not charge fees or housing costs.

The organization that standardizes rules and supplies guidance and leadership for winter guard activity is Winter Guard International (WGI). This group works with the circuit associations, judges' associations, and regional contests in North America and abroad. The WGI World Championship is held in April.

WGI contains several competition divisions. The Independent division A Class is for groups that are beginning programs, with younger members who have had limited opportunities to perform. The Open Class division is an intermediate level. The World Class has the most advanced programs and performers. There are also Scholastic divisions for units whose members come from the same school. The Scholastic divisions also include A Class, Open Class, and World Class categories.

Regional associations hold competitions as well. The Midwest Color Guard competitions involve guards from states such as Wisconsin, Illinois, Michigan, and Indiana. Localized competitions and exhibitions are followed by regional competitions, then circuit championships. For example, the winter guard from Irondale High School in New Brighton, Michigan, belongs to the North Star Color Guard Circuit. Since 1995 they have attended the WGI Midwest Regional, where they have been finalists since 1996. In 2002 they became the WGI Scholastic Open Class World Champions and were promoted to the Scholastic World Class division.

There are also Canadian-based associations such as the Canadian Winter Guard Association (CWA). This group's mission is "to promote and provide opportunities that will further the sport of pageantry arts, as well as provide a voice and common ground for interested individuals and groups." One well-known competition is the Calgary Stampede in Alberta, Canada. Canadian winter guards also participate in U.S. competitions. The Allegiance Elite, an Alberta winter guard, goes on a month-long competitive tour every summer through Canada and the United States. This group's guard was a finalist in the WGI Southwest Regional competitions the first time they competed there.

Many components go into a winter guard show. First, a general plan for the program has to be created. Then there is the choice of music. One show of the Avalon Winter Guard in Waukesha, Wisconsin focused on songs from the group Chicago. Independence Winter Guard from Tinley Park, Illinois has presented a program involving its members' lives and views of the world, using excerpts of famous people, music, and places from 1986 to the present. Groups use classical music, jazz, original music, and music that may surprise the spectators and get their attention.

When a performance is planned, all parts of the program are considered. This planning is called pacing. Where and when to use effects and how and why they will be performed must be taken into account. The music will create the mood or audience appeal. Therefore, it is important to consider who the audience is, what will

The pacing of a winter guard performance must take into account all parts of the program, including special effects, props, music, mood, and dance.

appeal to these people, and how they will respond to various musical selections. Not only is it important for the music to appeal to the spectators, it must also appeal to the winter guard members who will perform it. If they cannot relate to the music, its mood, message, or appeal, then they will not be able to present an effective program. The music's ending should also give the program a strong finish. Finally, the music needs to show off the winter guard's abilities by letting the group perform to its best advantage.

In addition to the personality of the guard, the concept and design of the performance play an important role. A program is not put together on a whim; on the contrary,

Winter guards design costumes, props, flats, and sets that complement their performance, often using color to help portray the mood or message of their performance.

there are writers for different needs, such as equipment and movement. The staff selects the music and works with the equipment and movement areas. They must take into account the speed and rhythm of the music, and make sure performers understand the actual timing of the music's sections.

The staging design must function effectively in both the program and the competition arena. It is an important part of the program's overall effect. Staging designs may be front stage, center stage, or a geometric line. Performers may all work in a small or "tight" area to create a mood or effect, or may be more open across the area for the same reasons. They may focus on the entire guard's moving together in unison for a musical section, then emphasize individual performers in a different section. Sometimes performers with different types of equipment interact during the music.

There are three basic approaches used to design a show: geometric drill, freeform design, and theatrical staging. Geometric drill uses basic forms such as circles and squares. Freeform design breaks up a line of performers into segments. Since any pathways used in the layout must be established, each individual's movements must be planned. Theatrical staging has entrances and exits, and it can focus on sections of the performers. The creation of a staging design has plenty of room for flexibility to tailor the performance so it is just right for the winter guard. The main point is that the writers and performers know everything about the show and how they want the audience to feel: surprised, but not confused, with unexpected effects at times and familiar effects, too. A successful design has balance, visual ideas that flow from one to another, staging so that one section of performers is not blocked by another, equipment whose space requirement has been adequately provided for, and intensity levels demonstrated through performer placement.

The requirements for a winter guard member include a strong work ethic. While the program is being planned and finalized, the winter guard members prepare to give a winning performance. Each technique that the guard will use needs to be taught and mastered. Although they receive training in practice sessions, winter guard performers must be willing to practice independently. Two three-hour classes per week over the course of a month may help the members gain the skills they need.

High school groups have after-school practices several hours a night and and on weekends. Independent groups may start at 8 A.M. and not finish until after midnight. Practice involves warm-up exercises so no one pulls a muscle during the routines. Sometimes a guard member gets hurt by equipment that was tossed poorly or not caught correctly. The only thing the injured person can do is keep working with that piece of equipment to be able to control it.

Once the basic skills are mastered, practice emphasizes refining technique. Instructors should be able to tell guard members why a move is being made and what its effect will be on the entire program, and answer any other questions on the execution of the moves. Once the performers understand the reasons and levels of a piece, they will be able to understand it emotionally and pass those emotions on to the audience.

During practice hair is pulled back. Proper shoes, along with clothing that allows movement, are worn. Performance time is a different situation. Often the performers still keep their hair pulled back, but now they will be wearing a variety of costumes. Some are loose and flowing like gowns; others are skin-hugging. The costumes enhance the performance by providing visual cues and setting the mood. Makeup is a major costume component. The exaggerated facial features resulting from the makeup help spectators appreciate the emotions and feelings the performers express.

Depending on the type of show design used, winter guard performers may form shapes like squares or circles, be broken into different segments, or exit and enter the stage during the performance.

The choreography, or the arrangement of a program's movements, is meant to interact with the audience. The spectators' knowledge and experiences blend with the movement to create audience reaction and interpretation. It is important that the performance relate to its viewers, but what those viewers think or feel because of what they see can be unique to each person. The choreographer creates mood in dance and different stage settings. The audience is then ready to experience the winter guard's performance and react to it.

In the late 1970s WGI began to hold its own competitions, then called the WGI Olympics. Twenty-nine guards competed in the first championship. By the third WGI championship in 1980, there were 60 guards from 14 states and one Canadian province competing in events such as Pass in Review and Standing Presentation of Colors.

Over time, dance was introduced to color and winter guard, and props, flats, and sets were added. The concept of winter guard as entertainment, not military formation, developed as theater and dance were incorporated.

Competitions are usually held on weekends. Winter guard circuits hold regional contests, which are stepping stones to participation in the WGI Championships. Teams are grouped by status (independent or scholastic), number of members, and general skill level, with the less-skilled groups performing first.

Judges train for their positions by taking courses, attending clinics, and sending in tapes of performances they have critiqued or judged to receive feedback on their judging. Judges have the same levels as the performers. Some are novices, some are intermediate in their judging experience, and some are advanced.

Judges time the length of the show, and members are observed as to whether or not they stayed in the performance boundaries. Judges also make sure equipment is legal and that the show's pace is appropriate. Judges look at the ensemble's movement and equipment. They also analyze the written design and group excellence of the product, and the general effect the program has on the audience, to assess if the program is effective in its communication skills.

Judging winter guard competition is a difficult job. The scoring decisions that judges make are scrutinized as closely as those made by a sports umpire or referee. Judges process thousands of bits of data over the course of each five-minute show. They will see many performances over the course of each day's competition, and have to be as alert and consistent in scoring the last performance of the day as they were for the first one. After watching a performance, judges may have only two minutes to check on regulations and assign a score. They also give suggestions to solve difficulties a guard may be having in a performance area. Judges, instructors, and fans watch the adjudication tapes to review the performance. After assessing approximately 30 presentations over a six-hour time frame, each judge then meets with the instructors to go over the day's competition.

BRINGING THE ARTS TO YOUR SCHOOL

Winter guard is one of the fastest growing pageantry arts. According to Winter Guard International, winter guard changes and evolves faster than any other pageantry-based activity. Today, winter guard often substitutes for the loss of many school-based arts programs. Winter Guard International's educational materials are used as the curriculum in many schools that offer classes in dance and guard equipment.

Winter guards earn points for general effect, performance, showmanship, physical motion/equipment coordination, marching and maneuvering, and carriage of equipment.

Several additional factors affect scores. A larger, higher-roofed facility can change the performance's impact because guard members may be more spread out over a larger area. A judging area that is crowded with fans on both sides, or a high or lower judging vantage point all have an impact on scoring. The judge's view will not be the same view most of the spectators have.

The Web site Silkonline.org sums up the winter guard experience:

Being part of a winter guard unit means making a commitment to a group of people, saying that you will work just as hard as they will to make the team as good as it can be. Above all, they learn that whatever you put forward is what you will get back, hard work pays off eventually and every person has it in them to achieve their goals.

WGI has expanded from 30 color guards to over 400 guard and percussion groups that compete over a period of three days at seven different sites. The WGI World Championships are attended by thousands of participants and continue to grow each year.

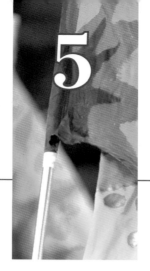

The Pageantry Arts

The spectator-pleasing programs of color guard and winter guard join with those of marching band, drum and bugle corps, dance and drill teams, cheerleading, pep squads, and baton twirlers to make up the pageantry arts. With their music, choreographed moves, equipment, and intensity of presentation, these activities combine artistic interpretation with athleticism to the extent that some of them, such as cheerleading, are sometimes referred to as sports.

Drill began in the United States in the late 1920s. Originally called pep squads, their moves showed military influence. Most pep squad participants were girls who

A twirler with the Purdue University Golden Girls performs with the university's marching band and dance team. Like color guards, baton twirlers are often part of marching bands.

wore uniforms of long pleated skirts and military-style blouses. These drill teams performed during halftime breaks at football games. As these teams grew in popularity, male participants performed gymnastic moves and women participants danced. Later, competitions began, including the Miss Dance and Drill Team USA Pageant. When an Australian drill team made a guest performance in the pageant, the idea for international drill team competition was born. In 1985 the international competition was hosted by Japan, the first time it was held abroad.

Cheerleading began in the late 1800s when seven men led a yell on the sidelines of a Princeton University football game. Later a Minnesota student got so excited he jumped in front of the crowd, and cheerleading began its journey toward pageantry art. Pom pon routines were begun in the 1930s, and when men became soldiers in World War II, women became the primary cheerleaders. The Baltimore Colts football team organized the first professional cheerleading squad in NFL history. Until then, high school squads had cheered at major league football games. In 1976 the Dallas Cowboys cheering squad became dancing cheerleaders. Junior high, high school, and collegiate cheerleading competitions began to be held, and national safety standards were set. These standards regulate the height of pyramids formed by cheerleaders and other gymnastic moves, such as tumbling, partner stunts, and jumps. In general, proper training, warm-up, stretching exercises, and spotting techniques are stressed.

A COLOR GUARD ON BROADWAY

The Star of Indiana Drum and Bugle Corps was formed in Bloomington, Indiana in 1984. The corps finished in the Top Ten at the Drum Corps International World Championships in its first year of competition and won more titles from 1990 to 1993 than any other corps.

In 1993, under the direction of James Mason, the group began its transformation from a 128-member drum corps to a theatrical show combining outdoor pageantry with the special effects of musical theater. The following year they toured with the Canadian Brass Quintet and began an indoor stage program called Brass Theater, which they performed in the United States.

In 1999 the musical production known as *Blast!* opened in London and then moved on to Broadway. According to Artistic Director James Mason, "This show traces our heritage of color guard, drum and bugle corps and marching band, concentrating primarily on the brass and percussion instruments, along with the use of what we call a 'visual ensemble' to interpret the music visually by spinning and manipulating props such as flags, rifles, and sabers. That's the traditional palette we work from. Then we take those elements and blend them all together while at the same time expanding the palette with dramatic lighting, intricate choreography, exciting costumes, and stage effects to enhance the show theatrically.

During *Blast!* the cast explores the power of color. As the colors become "warmer" in shade, corps members move from the stage into the audience to interact with the spectators. All aspects of the show were carefully chosen to show the emotional qualities of the colors. Different from anything that has ever been staged before, *Blast!* is truly a unique musical theater experience and has received rave reviews.

Indoor percussion is another one of the fastest-growing pageantry arts. Winter Guard International describes indoor percussion in this way: "Faces of performers are a study in concentration, hands a blur as they play musical notes fast and furious, and all the while with drums weighing upwards of 50 pounds in tow." These performances are beginning to be known as Percussion Theater because of their combination of musicianship, athleticism, and individual expression. Only percussion section instruments are permitted (with the exception of the string bass), and no taped music is allowed.

Two of the largest baton twirling associations today are the United States Twirling Association (USTA) and the National Baton Twirling Association. Each of them holds national competitions every year. The United States Twirling Association rotates the location of its competition to encourage participation by its entire membership. USTA Junior and Senior Men, Women, and Team winners represent the United States at the world competition hosted annually by the World Baton Twirling Federation.

At the World Championships, twirlers can compete in individual, pairs, and team events. Judges focus on technical merit (technique, speed, variety, difficulty, clearness, and sureness) and artistic expression, scoring on an Olympic scale of 1 to 10. Individual competitions have compulsory and freestyle moves. Pairs and team competitions are similar to the freestyle, but they also include partner or team interaction, unison, and baton exchanges.

Canadian twirler Hollie Neilson is a good example of how skill and talent pay off. After winning the Junior Women's World Freestyle Championships twice, she moved up to the Senior division (ages 15 and older) and won the Senior Women's World Championship. "This one meant more because the competitors had so much more experience," she said. Hollie is only the third person to win this division in her first year of Senior competition.

Pageantry arts have been highlighted on television, in the movies, and on Broadway. The documentary *Hard Corps* follows the life of a young man from New York City as he performs with the Cadets Drum and Bugle Corps of Bergenfield, New Jersey over an eight-year period, until he "ages out" at 21. During the summer, the Cadets entertain hundreds of thousands of fans as they travel over 20,000 miles throughout the United States. This video shows portions of various competitions.

The movie *Drumline* focuses on another young man from New York City who is recruited to attend a fictional university in Georgia, Atlanta A&T University. He may have difficulty fitting in socially, but his drumming talents are his key to marching band success.

No matter what type of performance they pursue, pageantry arts performers feel a sense of family and accomplishment. Blue Devils color guard member Jennifer Byers summed up her feelings:

My experiences with the Blue Devils color guard have been life-altering. Without them, I would never appreciate the true meaning of hard work. You learn to push yourself

"The pageantry arts" is an umbrella term that refers to performance groups like color and winter guards, marching bands, drum corps, percussion units, dance and drill teams, and baton twirlers.

beyond your limits, even when you don't think that you can go any further. Above all, I value the friendships that I have made along the way. The people that I love and hold closest to my heart are those that I have met in the past five years as a member of the Blue Devils color guard. These are the memories that I have made, and the lessons that I have learned—both of which I will take with me for the rest of my life.

A guard's performance is limited only by the imagination, dedication, and skill of its members. From the battlefield to the playing field to the Broadway stage, color guard as a pageantry art continues to develop and to astound audiences. At the same time, guard participants continue to gain skills, friendships, personal satisfaction, and team spirit.

Glossary

adjudication tapes – Videotapes used by judges to review a group's performance during competition.

alumni – Former members of a group, such as a color guard or other organization.

auxiliary – A supplemental or assisting group.

band front – Another name for an auxiliary of the marching band or drum corps, such as color guards, pom squads, and twirlers.

baton – A hollow metal rod twirled by drum majors or majorettes.

brass section – Bugles and other brass instruments in a drum corps or marching band.

choreography – The arrangement of the movements in a program.

color-bearer – A person who carries and presents the national flag.

color guard – A component of a marching band or drum corps that entertains spectators mainly through the use of flags, rifles, and sabers.

drum corps (also called drum and bugle corps) – A pageantry arts group with a military history. Drum corps combine marching with percussion and brass instruments and color guard.

drum major – The leader of a marching band, the drum major often holds or twirls a baton.

drumline – The percussion section of a drum corps or marching band.

ensemble – A small group singing or playing music together.

flags – Another term for color guard members.

freeform design – An approach to show design that breaks performers into segments, planning the movements of individual performers.

freestyle – A category of competition that is not limited to a specified style or pattern of movement.

geometric drill – An approach to show design using basic forms such as circles and squares.

guidons – Flags used to mark the intervals between color guard company squads.

majorette – A woman who leads a marching band while twirling a baton.

pageantry arts – General term used to describe different performance groups such as color guard, winter guard, drum corps, dance/drill teams, and marching bands. The pageantry arts are also referred to as the performing arts.

pennons – Small flags that were placed on the lances of medieval knights.

percussion – Instruments such as drums and cymbals which must be struck to produce a sound.

rifles – Term for the wooden guns twirled by color and winter guards as part of their performance.

saber (also spelled sabre) – A modified sword used in color guard and winter guard performances.

silk(s) – Another term for the flags used by guard members; silks can also be used to refer to the guard members themselves.

spinning – The action of performing with, and twirling, flags.

theatrical staging – An approach to show design that uses entrances and exits, allowing the focus to be on different performers or the characters they portray.

twirler – A person who performs with a baton.

winter guard – A type of indoor performance that uses color guard equipment (flags, rifles, sabers, etc.) and taped music.

Internet Resources

http://www.dci.org

Drum Corps International establishes rules and regulations for drum and bugle corps. The DCI Web site tells the history of drum corps, offers competition information, and provides links to many individual drum corps.

http://www.ncbaonline.org

The Web site of the Northern California Band Association offers information on competition rules, including judging criteria for color guards and other auxiliaries.

http://www.tob.org

The Tournament of Bands provides performance opportunities in field band (including color guards), indoor guard, majorette, percussion, and dance team, for middle school, junior high, high school, college, and university students.

http://www.wgasc.org

The Winter Guard Association of Southern California offers information on area groups, judging, scholarships, and more.

http://www.winterguard.ca

The Canadian Winter Guard Association (CWA) is the information site for Canadian competitions, guards, camps, and events, and includes links to many Canadian groups.

http://www.wgi.org

Winter Guard International establishes rules and regulations for winter guard. Their Web site contains competition information and links to other guard sites.

http://worldofpageantry.com

World of Pageantry is a pageantry arts Web site with news on groups and competitions and links to other pageantry arts sites.

Further Reading

Bailey, Wayne, and Thomas Caneva. *The Complete Marching Band Resource Manual.* Philadelphia: University of Pennsylvania Press, 1994.

Garty, Judy. *Marching Band Competition.* Philadelphia, Pennsylvania: Mason Crest Publishers, 2003.

Garty, Judy. *Techniques of Marching Bands.* Philadelphia, Pennsylvania: Mason Crest Publishers, 2003.

Holston, Kim R. *The Marching Band Handbook.* Jefferson, North Carolina: McFarland & Company, 1994.

Sloan, Karyn. *Techniques of Color Guard.* Philadelphia, Pennsylvania: Mason Crest Publishers, 2003.

Vickers, Steve. *A History of Drum and Bugle Corps.* Madison, Wisconsin: Sights and Sounds, Inc., 2002.

Index

PICTURE CREDITS

Front cover: Photosport

Back cover: Courtesy of Purdue University Golden Silks/Photo by Sara Suppinger

Associated Press/Wide World Photos: 6; Tim Jackson Photography: 36; Courtesy of Amanda Brown: 9 Courtesy of the Marine Military Academy: 14; Courtesy of Purdue University: 52; Ron Walloch Performance Photography: 2, 12, 16, 20, 23, 24, 27, 30, 33, 38, 43, 44, 47, 50, 58; Photo from the Collection of John W. Ziemann: 19.

TERRY USILTON teaches English at Easton High School in Easton, Maryland. She writes for children's publications and is a consultant for the Southern Regional Education Board. She has a great deal of respect for the dedication shown by pageantry arts participants.